Library of Congress Cataloging-in-Publication Data

Iverson, Janice L.

   As a Woman/by Janice L Iverson—1st ed

   ISBN-13: 978-0692861400

   ISBN-10: 0692861408

As a Woman

Peace in the Pieces

Dr Janice L Iverson

Introduction

Every woman has her own unique story to tell about harassment and abuse in the workplace and on the home front. For years, I, like other women, remained silent. I was left alone to grapple with the shame, guilt, and self doubt. I tried to make sense of what had happened, tried to forget it and put it behind me. But as hard as I tried it was always there tearing at my sense of self and self worth. It took me a long time to reconcile what had happened to me and reclaim all the pieces of myself and find peace again.

On the following pages I hope to remind you who you are, help you reclaim your truth, and find peace in the pieces of your own story. You are strong, you are deserving, and you have value and worth. The words are simple and stand for themselves. The story behind them is yours to be told . . . to be filled in on the empty pages as declaration of your own truth. The first step or the last to reclaiming all of who you are.

I have the right to be honest with myself and live my life completely . . .

Utilizing all of my gifts,

skills, and talents

to the best of my ability.

I *have the right to be treated*
with respect by all for
who I am . . .
not for who you want me to be.

I have the right to have my own opinion, to express it freely, without concern of reprisal, or patronization, or humiliation ...

To have the respect I deserve as a person with intelligence, self worth, and a voice worthy of being heard.

I *have the right to say no.*

To be angry,

to cry tears of joy,

and sadness . . .

at the same time

I have the right to be

loved just as I am

To decry false images of women
and reject being stereotyped.

I have the right to break through the glass ceiling.

*To have certainty of my own worth
and pursue the fulfillment
of my own needs.*

I have the right to

change my mind

To excel beyond   .   .   .

to search for more

To Never Quit

To Quit

To start again.

I have the right

to peace of mind . . .

To harmony in life . . .

as a spiritual being

To be unafraid

and unrestrained

38

Free to seek and find

a better life . . .

A kinder world . . .

42

And

Unconditional Love

About the Author

Dr. Janice Iverson earned a PhD in Psychology and is a Licensed Professional Clinical Counselor. She was the founder and owner of the Family Center for Understanding counseling center working with adolescents, women, and couples. She has a fifteen year career in academia as an assistant professor, program chair, and vice president of academic affairs. Her teaching interests focused on the psychology of women, gender, and adjustment.

A Minnesota native (who calls Savannah, Georgia her soul home) Iverson currently lives in Parrish, Florida with her husband, Eugene,, and their dog Crosby. She is so proud to be the mom of Sally and Jesse who have made her life complete in ways she never knew possible.

Iverson is the author of As A Woman: Piece in the Pieces (2017). She is currently working on her next book release, The Fantastic Journey of Self Discovery.

www.ingramcontent.com/pod-product-compliance
Lightning Source LLC
Chambersburg PA
CBHW031342040426
42443CB00006B/449